DENNIS ALEXANDER'S
FAVORITE SOLOS
7 OF HIS ORIGINAL PIANO SOLOS

FOREWORD

Each year Alfred publishes a variety of sheet music solos for students at various levels. Teachers and students use them for recitals, auditions, festivals, or just to have fun. Many of these become student favorites, and teachers continue to teach them through the years.

Just as teachers and students have their own preferences, the composers who write these solos also have their own personal favorites. For the Composer's Choice series, the editors at Alfred asked each composer to choose his or her best-loved sheet music solos that had been published through the years and compile them into graded collections for students. They were asked to reflect upon when they had written the pieces and see if the music evoked strong feelings or conjured up treasured memories. In addition, they considered the inspiration behind the pieces, students who had studied the music, or comments that they had received from teachers about the solos.

As a result of this process, Alfred is pleased to introduce Dennis Alexander's *Favorite Solos*, Book 3, a collection of seven late intermediate to early advanced solos for students of all ages. Students, teachers and audiences will enjoy the variety of styles, sounds and moods of this music. We feel sure that Dennis's *Favorite Solos* will quickly become your favorites, too. Enjoy!

CONTENTS

Alfred

Commissioned by the Billings, Montana
Music Teachers Association, November 1992

Danse Humoresque

Dennis Alexander

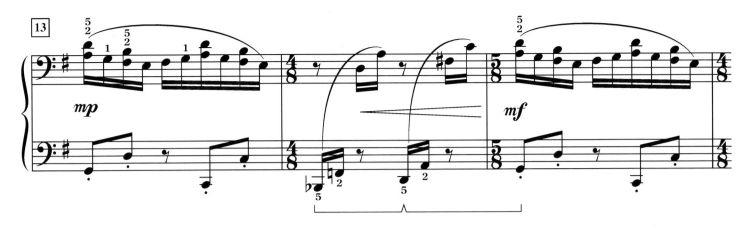

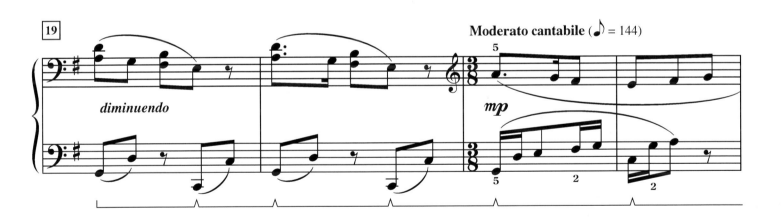

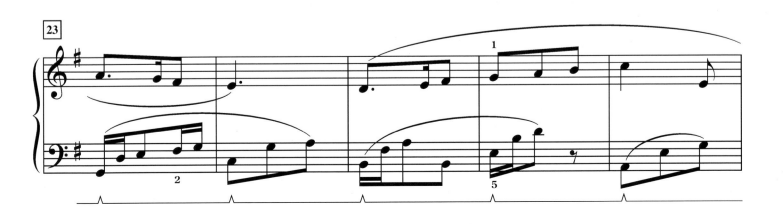

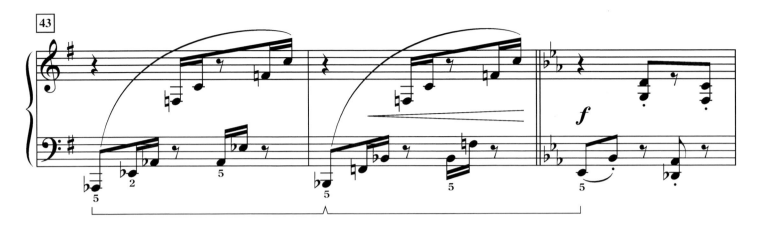

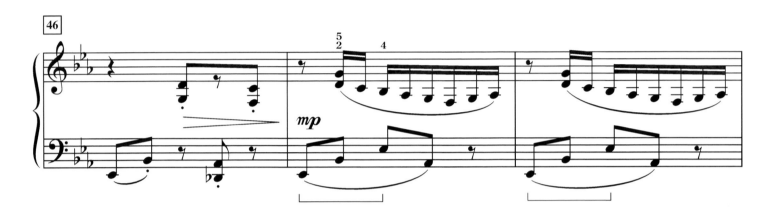

Dedicated to the Puyallup Valley Chapter
Washington State Music Teachers Association
November, 1998

Reverie in F Minor

Dennis Alexander

Serenade in E-flat Major

Dennis Alexander

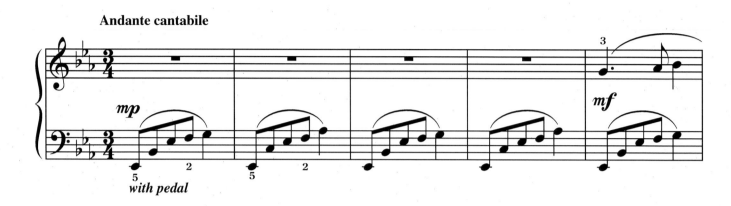

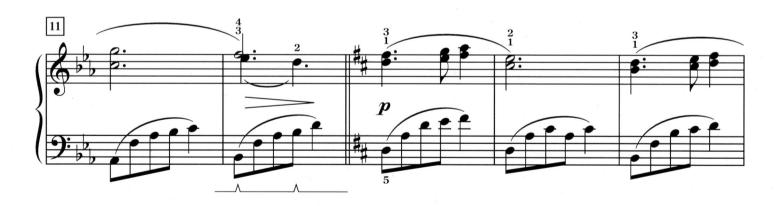

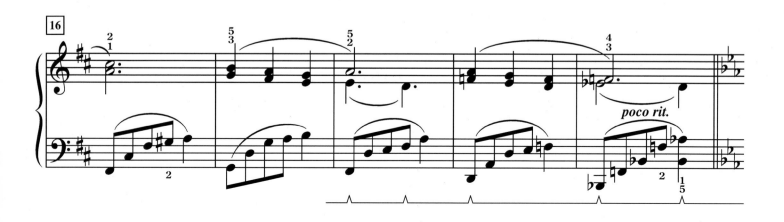

12

Tarantella Burleska

Dennis Alexander

Toccata Spirito

Dennis Alexander

18

Smooth Talker

Dennis Alexander

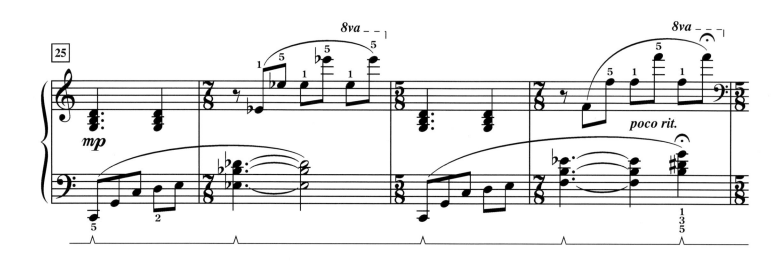

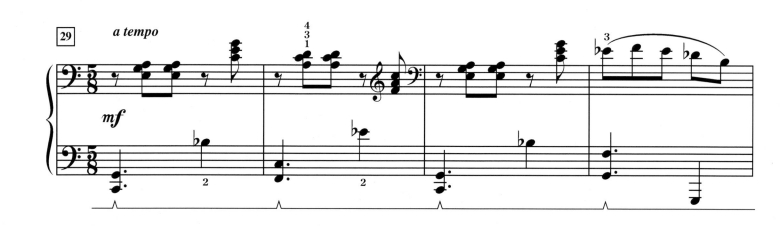

calando e poco a poco rit.

Commissioned by the Double Sharp Music Club, Warroad, Minnesota,
in memory of Katie Jo Olafson

Journey of the Heart

Dennis Alexander